Mount Rushmore

Lola Schaefer

Heinemann Library
Chicago, Illinois

© 2002 Heinemann Library,
an imprint of Capstone Global Library, LLC
Chicago, IL

Customer Service 888-454-2279

Visit our website at www.heinemannlibrary.com

Designed by Depke Design
Printed and bound in the United States of America, North Mankato, MN

15 14 13
11 10 9

Library of Congress Cataloging-in-Publication Data
Schaefer, Lola M., 1950

    Mount Rushmore / Lola Schaefer.

      p. cm. -- (Symbols of Freedom)

    Includes bibliographical references (p.) and index

    ISBN 978-1-58810-176-1 (1-58810-176-2) (HC), 978-1-58810-397-0 (1-58810-397-8) (Pbk)

      1. Mount Rushmore National Memorial (S.D.)--Juvenile literature. [1. Mount Rushmore National Memorial (S.D.). 2. National monuments.] I. Title. II. Series.

F657.R8 S33 2001
978.3'93--dc21

                                                     2001001631

Acknowledgments
The author and publishers are grateful to the following for permission to reproduce copyright material:
Cover photograph: Richard T. Notwitz/Corbis
p. 4 Richard T. Notwitz/Corbis; p. 5 Randy Wells/Corbis; p. 6 Phil Schermeister/Corbis; p. 7 L.Clarke/Corbis; p. 8 Lester Lefkowitz/The Stock Market; p. 9 PhotoDisc; pp. 11, 12, 13, 20, 22, 27 Underwood & Underwood/Corbis; pp. 14, 16, 17, 23, 24 Bettmann/Corbis; p. 15 National Archives and Records Administration; pp. 18, 21 Corbis; p. 19 Craig Brown/Index Stock; pp. 25, 26 AP Photo; p. 28 Greg Latza/AP Photo; p. 29 Dave Bartruff/Corbis

Special thanks to James G. Popovich, Chief of Interpretation and Visitors Service, Mount Rushmore National Memorial, for his help in the preparation of this book.

Every effort has been made to contact copyright holders of any material reproduced in this book. Any omissions will be rectified in subsequent printings if notice is given to the publisher.

Some words are shown in bold, **like this.** You can find out what they mean by looking in the glossary.

072013
007558RP

Contents

Faces of America's Past

Mount Rushmore National **Memorial** is a group of stone carvings. It is in the **Black Hills** of South Dakota. The carvings are **symbols**. They help us remember important men in America's past.

The faces on the mountain **honor** four
United States presidents. They are George
Washington, Thomas Jefferson, Theodore
Roosevelt, and Abraham Lincoln. Each
face is as tall as a five-story building.

Visiting Mount Rushmore

Millions of people visit Mount Rushmore every year. The Mount Rushmore National Park has a museum, visitors' center, gift shop, hiking trail, and theaters.

Visitors can walk the Presidential Trail. This trail leads them along the base at the front of the mountain. Visitors stop on decks to look at the carvings.

Looking at Mount Rushmore

Mount Rushmore is made of a rock called **granite**. It is light gray in color. Sometimes the rock looks pink during the sunrise.

Helicopter rides help visitors see Mount Rushmore from the air. At night, lights shine on the **memorial**. The lights make the carvings glow.

# A Big Idea

In the 1920s, a group of people from South Dakota had an idea. They wanted people to visit their state. They decided to build a **memorial**. They wanted it to **honor** American heroes.

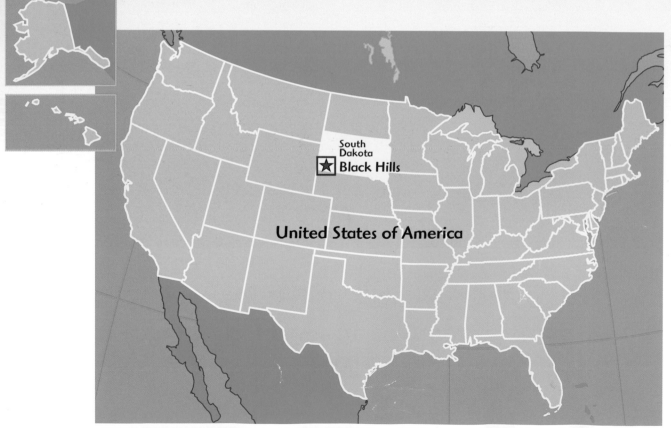

South Dakota
★ Black Hills

United States of America

They chose a **sculptor** named Gutzon Borglum to make the memorial. He was a famous American artist.

The Perfect Spot

Borglum visited the **Black Hills** of South Dakota. He looked at many mountains. He studied the shapes of the rocks. He watched how the sun shone on them.

In 1925, he and his son Lincoln chose Mount Rushmore. This would be the place for the **memorial**. Borglum was excited to begin work in the Black Hills.

A Different Plan

The people who planned the **memorial** wanted Borglum to carve heroes of the old west. They were thinking of someone like **Buffalo Bill Cody.**

George Washington

Thomas Jefferson

Abraham Lincoln

Theodore Roosevelt

But Borglum wanted to carve the heads of
people who were important to all Americans.
He chose four U.S. presidents. They had
changed America for the better.

Borglum chose George Washington because he was a great leader and the first president of the United States. Thomas Jefferson was important because he wrote the **Declaration of Independence**.

Borglum chose Abraham Lincoln because he was president during the **Civil War**. He also helped free the slaves. Theodore Roosevelt built the **Panama Canal** for world trade.

Some People Disagree

Many people did not agree with carving faces on Mount Rushmore. They had different reasons for not wanting the **memorial** built.

18

Some people thought the project would cost too much money and never be finished. **Native Americans** believed that people should not change the beauty of the **Black Hills.**

Work Begins

In 1927, Borglum began work on Mount Rushmore. At first, work was slow. Borglum and his **crew** always needed more money and supplies.

Borglum chose to make George Washington's face in the mountain first. He began carving Washington's head on the highest **cliff**.

Work Goes On

After Washington's face was carved, the **crew** began on President Jefferson. Thomas Jefferson's head was completed in 1936. The project was halfway finished.

Next, work began on Presidents Lincoln and Roosevelt. To carve President Roosevelt's head, much rock had to be blasted away.

Many Workers

Borglum's **crew** had 400 people. Some workers were "call boys." They took orders to men up and down the mountain. Others were stonecutters who cut and polished stone.

Most workers were drillers. These men carved the stone. Drillers were lowered next to the mountain by a **cable**. They hung high above the ground.

Finishing Mount Rushmore

Borglum put his son Lincoln in charge of the project. The **crew** worked through the cold winter. In July of 1939, all four heads were carved.

For two more years, workers put the final touches on the **memorial**. In 1941, Mount Rushmore was finished. The memorial we see today looks the same as it did then.

Protecting Mount Rushmore

Today, workers repair the stone to **protect** it. The **granite** moves in cold and hot weather. This makes the stone crack. Workers fix the cracks.

Workers also clean the stone. They remove plants that grow on the **memorial**. Visitors will enjoy a clean and safe Mount Rushmore for many years.

Fact File

Mount Rushmore

★ Rock weighing 450,000 tons was removed to create the faces on Mount Rushmore. This is the same weight as 8,200 African elephants.

★ No workers were killed during the building of Mount Rushmore. There were several broken bones, cuts, and bruises.

★ The **Black Hills** are thought to be **holy** ground by the **Sioux** people. They believe this is where the world was created. Today they still have hope that their land will be returned to them.

★ The workers who made Mount Rushmore made 50 or 60 cents an hour.

Glossary

Black Hills group of hills in the Harney Range located in the southwest corner of the state of South Dakota

Buffalo Bill Cody well-known buffalo hunter, soldier, and owner of a "Wild West" show in the 1800s

cable thick wire or rope

Civil War U.S. war in the 1800s, in which northern states fought against southern states

cliff high, steep rock face

crew team of people who work together on a job

Declaration of Independence paper that says that America is a separate country from Britain

granite hard gray rock often used as a building material

holy special place or thing that has to do with what a person believes about God

honor to do something that shows great respect for someone or something

memorial building or statue that helps us remember a person or an idea

Native American one of the original peoples who lived in North and South America or a descendant of these people

Panama Canal man-made waterway through the country of Panama that is a shortcut for ships from the Atlantic to the Pacific Ocean

protect to keep safe

sculptor person who makes statues and carvings

Sioux group of Native American Indians who live in the northern Great Plains and in southern Canada

symbol something that stands for an idea

More Books to Read

Curlee, Lynn. *Rushmore*. New York: Scholastic Press, 1999.

Doherty, Craig and Katherine. *Mt. Rushmore*. Woodbridge, Conn.: Blackbirch Press, 1995. An older reader can help you with this book.

Santella, Andrew. *Mount Rushmore*. Danbury, Conn.: Children's Press, 1999. An older reader can help you with this book.

Index